EDWARD DORN

GUNSLINGER 1 & 2

Fulcrum Press

ACKNOWLEDGEMENTS

To *The North Atlantic Turbine* (Fulcrum 1967), *Gunslinger Book 1* (Black Sparrow 1968), *Gunslinger Book 2* (Black Sparrow 1969).

This edition first published 1969.

BOOK 1

The curtain might rise
anywhere on a single speaker

I met in Mesilla
The Cautious Gunslinger
of impeccable personal smoothness
and slender leather encased hands
folded casually
to make his knock.
He would show you his map.
There is your domain.
Is it the domicile it looks to be
or simply a retinal block
of seats in,
he will flip the phrase
the theater of impatience.

     If it is where you are,
the footstep in the flat above
in a foreign land
or any shimmer the city
sends you
the prompt sounds
of a metropolitan nearness
     he will unroll the map of love.
His knock resounds
inside its own smile, where?
I ask him is my heart.

Not this pump he answers
artificial already and bound
touching me
with his leathern finger
as the Queen of Hearts burns
from his gauntlet into my eyes.

    Flageolets of fire
he says there will be.
This is for your sadly missing heart
the girl you left
in Juarez, the blank
political days press her now
in the narrow abode
confines of the river town
her dress is torn
by the misadventure of
        her gothic search
The mission bells are ringing
in Kansas.
Have you left something out :
Negative, says my Gunslinger,
no *thing* is omitted.

I held the reins of his horse
while he went off into the desert
to pee. *Yes,* he reflected
when he returned, that's better.
How long, he asked
have you been in this territory.
Years I said. Years.
Then you will know where we can have
a cold drink before sunset and then a bed
will be my desire if you can find one
for me, I have no wish to continue
my debate with men,
my mare lathers with tedium

her hooves are dry
Look they are covered with the alkali
of the enormous space
between here and formerly.
Need I repeat, we have come
without sleep from Nuevo Laredo.
And why do you have a female horse
Gunslinger? I asked. Don't move
he replied
the sun rests deliberately
on the rim of the sierra.

And where will you now I asked.
Five days northeast of here
depending of course on whether one's horse
is of iron or flesh
there is a city called Boston
and in that city there is a hotel
whose second floor has been let
to an inscrutable Texan named Hughes
Howard? I asked
The very same.
And what do you mean by inscrutable,
         oh Gunslinger?
I mean to say that he
has not been seen since 1833.

But when you have found him my Gunslinger
what will you do, oh what will you do?
You would not know
that the souls of old Texans
are in jeopardy in a way not common
to other men, young man.

You would not know
of the long plains night
where they carry on

and arrange their genetic duels
with men of other states —
so there is a longhorn bull half mad
half deity
who awaits an account from me
back of the sun you nearly disturbed
just then. Here, hold my mare
I must visit the cactus once more
and then, we'll have that drink.

STRUM
strum
  And by that sound
we had come there, false fronts
my Gunslinger said make
the people mortal
and give their business
an inward cast. They cause culture.
Honk HONK, Honk HONK
that sound comes
at the end of the dusty street,
where we meet the gaudy Madam
of that very cabaret going in
where our drink is to be drunk —
  Hello there, *Slinger!* Long time
no see
what brings you, who's your friend,
to these parts, and where
if you don't mind my asking, *Hello,*
are you headed.
Boston! you don't say, Boston
is an actionable town they say
never been there myself
but I've had some nice girls
from up Boston way
turned out real *spunky* they did
But you look like you

always did Slinger, you
still make me shake, I mean
why do you think I've got my hand on
my hip if not to *steady* myself
and the way I twirl this
Kansas City parasol
if not to keep the dazzle
of them spurs outa my eyes
Miss Lil! I intervened
you mustn't slap my
Gunslinger on the back
in such an off hand manner
I think the sun, the moon
and some of the stars are
kept in their tracks
by this Person's equilibrium
or at least I sense some effect
on the perigee and appogee of all
our movements in this, I can't quite say,
man's presence, the setting sun's
attention I would allude to
and the very appearance
of his neurasthenic mare
lathered, as you can see, with abstract fatigue
Shit, Slinger! you still got that bitchy
old nag, and *who* is this
funny talker, you pick him up
in some sludgey seat of higher
learnin, Creeps! you always did
hang out with some curious refugees.
Anyway come up and see me
and bring your friend, anytime
if you're gonna be in town we
got an awful lot to talk about
for instance, remember that man
you was always looking for
name of Hughes?

Howard? I asked
You got it — that was
the gent's first handle
a texas dynamiter he was
back in '32
always turned my girls on a lot
when he blew in
A man in the house
is worth 2 in the street
anyday, like I say this
Hughes had a kind of interest
about him namely
a saddle bag full of currency
which don't hurt none
you remember there was this
trick called her Jane
you was sweet on her
got religion later and dropped
out, but I heard this Hughes
Howard? I asked
Right, boy
they say he moved to Vegas
or *bought Vegas* and
                    moved it.
I can't remember which.
Anyway, I remember you had
what your friend here
might call an obsession
about the man
don't tell me you're
still looking for him
I mean they say,
can't prove it by me,
Hughes —
Howard? I asked
Hey Slinger you better shut
that boy up!

Cut it, my friend
I was just —
Drop it!
Anyway, they say
this Howard is kinda
peculiar about bein seen
like anywhere anytime
sort of a spooky type
like a lota texans I know
plumb strange the way
they operate.
You know,
I had to deal with a texan once
nearly drove one of my best girls insane
insisted on her playing black jack
with his stud horse
who was pretty good
held the cards with his hooves
real articulate like and could add
fastern most humans
recall before I put a stop to it
we had special furniture
brought in from Topeka.
That horse would sit at
the table all night, terrible
on whiskey and rolled
a fair smoke
and this texan insisted he was
payin for my girl's time
and he could use it any way he
saw fit
as long as he was payin like
and I had to explain
a technical point to that Shareholder namely,
that he was paying for
her *ass,* which is not time!
How did you get rid of him

I asked
Well boy, that was singular
you know I thought and thought
and I was plum stumpt
that is,
until one of my regulars of the time
who had an interest in this girl
can't recall her *name*
but you'd know the fella
a wrangler from wyoming, THE Word
his name was
anyway he suggested we
turn that horse on —
Hughes? I asked.
Jesus! Slinger can't you *do*
something about that refugee
no! his mother was religious
so we turned this stud on
and it took most of a tampico
shipment to do the job
but I'll tell you Slinger
that horse laughed all that
night and they carried
him out next morning
and put him on the stage
for Amarillo, him and
the texan sittin in there all alone
and that horse was tellin everybody
what to do
Get that strong box up there,
get them "horses" hitched up
he'd say
rollin a big tampico bomber with his hooves
his shoes had come off, you see,
and he could do it so
natural anyway
and then he'd kinda *lounge*

inside the stage coach and
lean out the window winkin
at the girls, showing
his teeth, I can't say he was
unattractive, something kinda
handsome about his big face
and suggestive he was
a sorta manner
he had
    He kept sayin Can You Manage?
and Thank You!
every time the hostler hitched up
another horse
and then he had a kinda what
you might call a *derisive* air
when he'd say "Due In On Monday"
because you see it was Sunday
when they left town, but
he kept knockin his right hoof
against the inside of the coach
sayin You All Alright Out There?
and he had the texan's hat on
a stetson XX sorta cockwise
on his head it was
I tell you Slinger you would of
split your levis and dropped your
beads to seen it.

        Because he
was sayin some of the abstractest
things you ever heard
like Celery Is Crisp!
and we ain't seen him
or that individual texan
who owned him since.
I swear that stud must have become
a congressman or something since then

he sure was going strong on that
fresh Tampico — Some of the hands
that was there that day in fact
claimed he didn't leave on the stage
at all, there's still people
around here who'll claim that horse
flew back west when the texan
went to sleep 5 miles out of
town.
Where were we I asked,
when I noticed my Gunslinger
had retired to a shady spot
cast by the town's one cottonwood
Hold on, requested the Gunslinger
and held a conference to the side
with Lil

and then he kissed with a smile
her hand and she said you boys
enjoy yourself I'll see about you
later.
then as we mounted the steps
of the cabaret
The Gunslinger sang

> Oh a girl there was in the street
> the day we rode into La Cruz
> and the name of the name of her feet
> was the same as the name of the street
> and she stood and she stared like a moose
> and her hair was tangled and loose . . .

STRUM, strum

Do you know said the Gunslinger
as he held the yellow tequilla up
in the waning light of the cabaret

that this liquid is the last
dwindling impulse of the sun
and then he turned and knelt
and faced that charred orb
as it rolled below the swinging doors
as if it were entering yet descending
and he said to me No!
it is not.   It is that
cruelly absolute sign my father
I am the son of the sun, we two
are always in search
of the third — who is that I asked
Hughes?
Howard?
Yes.
No.
Why not?
Because the third can never be
a texan
Never?
Yes.
Why not?
I told you, back there
when you held my horse.
Ah.   if that is the case then
is your horse the Turned On
Horse of whom we've just now heard
and if that may be true how is it

your horse is also that
magnificently nervous mare
I've back there held?   Back there?
what is it you ask?
Is that your horse and was it
the Turned On Horse.
Possibly.
Possibly!   what do you mean?

No, my horse is not a texan.
What?
Drink the yellow sun
of your tequilla and calm
yourself, refugee
and then I shall tell you
because you are inattentive
and expect reason to follow
as some future chain gang does
a well worn road.
Look, by the way, a fight
has started, order again
before the place is smashed

      I then did order, yet
wondered, the inexplicability
of all that had, in this half
hour passed. And when
the divine tequillas were served
we two had retired to a table
obscure in the corner.
    Lo que pasa he breathed
this place is
in the constructive process
of ruin —
tables upended, the flak
of chips and drink surrounds us.

      But yet my Gunslinger
in his steady way deliberated
on the scene before us — Note
he said
that confusion.
I did.
What do you see
he asked.
Men fighting I answered

18

Is that all, he asked
Do you want the details
I asked
Don't be evasive he replied
What is the *principle* of what
you see.
I was hard put to understand this
I tried.
The principle, I said
is leverage. Not quite
the Gunslinger rejoined,
that is the mechanism
I asked for the principle.
Yes you did, quite plainly
said I
But I am afraid I —
Never mind he said, are these
men men.
Yes I answered on the heated margin
of that general battle
Is my horse a horse? he continued
I'm on that score not sure
I said.
Your horse seems different
from these men.
Quite right
but that's not altogether
what I am getting at. Here
he said, passing me the cigarette.
I think, he added
of taking you to Las Vegas.
Then you aren't going
to Boston. Not now he
exhaled, fresh distortions
as you yourself heard
have reached my ears.
Uh-huh I managed to exhale.

Thus we sat and still
I knew not the principle
of which he spoke.

STRUM, strum

Then there was an interlude
in which the brawl before our
indented eyes went on.
Auto-destruction he breathed
and I in that time was
suspended
as if in some margin of the sea
I saw the wading flanks
of horses spread in energy

What makes?
he suddenly asked in the smoke
and turmoil, and the bullets
flying,
What makes you think
oh what makes you
that this horse sitting between us
and who has not spoken
a word
or is it that I have
from the beginning
misjudged you.
The Horse grinned at me
Oh my Gunslinger, I said
If this be true
and it must be
because I can see in this horse
the Horse described
Will it not be very inappropriate
that Lil see this same Horse
in her establishment?

What of the girls?
Why, untaught refugee
do you think I have arranged
this mass collision, standard in its design
you see raging not 15 feet away
but to distract the vision
of that unpredictable crone?
She seemed nice enough to me
I said.
You have not lived 2000
and more years and as he
disengaged his eyes from mine
he said And speaking of said
Lady here, she, comes —

        My god, Slinger, she said
I am at your service,
replied the Gunslinger.
Oh knock that off!
I've got a business to tend to
and the smoke in this corner
is blinding besides, say
haven't I met that Horse
before? The Horse
rose from his chair and
tipped his stetson XX
Hello Lil, it's been a long time
here have a seat,
we've got a lot to talk
about, *Slow down*
the Gunslinger said and
that was the only time
I ever heard anybody speak
obliquely to the Horse.

        Thus sat the four of us
at last a company it seemed

and the Bombed Horse took off his stetson
XX, and drew on the table
our future course.

Whispered, as I did, aside
to the Gunslinger, Who, finally,
is this gaudy Lil? Lil,
I didn't expect to see
here — we were in Smyrna
together, now called Izmir
when they burned the place
down, we were
very young then
I lost touch of my old compadre Keys in that town
a mohawk valley boy
whose mother knew him
as "Sandy" and
who figured in several lives
of that time and
the periods since,
I might add. Does that
satisfy you?
Yes I answered.

    And then
the Oblique Horse
having waited patiently
for the course of that aside
to run
asked Have you finished.
It occurred to me
I might not readily
answer a horse
but I was discouraged
in whatever question
I might have felt
when the Gunslinger

on my arm put
the pressure of his leatherbound
fingers and gave me
a look
in the aftermath of those bullets
and that dispersing smoke
which said, Quietly.

STRUM, strum

          Then sat we amid aftermath
and those unruly customers in Lil's
cabaret and the Plugged In Horse
covered the table
with his elaborate plans
and as he planned he rolled
immense bombers
from the endless Tampico
in his saddle bags.
What's happened to my black ace
the Horse inquired
scraping his chair, reaching
under the table,
smiling, passing at the same time
his bomber without limit to me.
But, I,
don't recognize
this size,
it is, beyond, me.
No, mortal, that size is beyond your conception
Smoke. Don't describe yourself.
That's right, refugee, the Horse
thinks he's makin telescopes
pass it ! Hey Slinger !
Lil continued
Play some music.
Right, breathed the Gunslinger

and he looped toward the juke then, in a trajectory
of exquisite proportion a half dollar
which dropped home
as the 44 presented itself in the proximity
of his hand and interrogated the machine

A28, Joe Turner *Early in the Mornin'*
came out and lay on the turntable
His inquisitive 44 repeated the question
        and B13 clicked
Lightnin' Hopkins *Happy Blues for John Glenn,*
        and so on
the terse trajectories of silver then
the punctuations of his absolute 44
without even pushing his sombrero off his eyes
Gawddamit Slinger! there you
go wreckin my Wurlitzer again
sittin there
in that tipped back chair
can't you go *over* to the machine
and *put* the money in and *push*
the button like a normal bein?
them things cost money
and besides that Slinger, some
of these investors
is gettin edgy
since this Stoned Horse come in
they're talkin bout closin my place
down
scarin my girls with hostile talk.
My bartender gettin bugged
more *every time* you do some shit
like that.
Don't bring me down Lil,
we'll be out of here by and by.

Yea Lil, drop it

the Stoned Horse said.
We'd all rather *be* there
than talk about it.
It's all right Lil, I
said. Oh refugee
you talk like a natural
mortal, take your hand
off my knee
I've got other things to do
now.

STRUM

Just then a Drifter carrying
a divine guitar
passed by our table and the guise
inlaid around the string cut hole
pulsated as do
stars in the ring
of a clear night
Hi! Digger
the drifting guitarist greeted
the Bombed Horse
who was in his saddle bags
rummaging
Heidigger? I asked
the Xtian statistician
is that who you are?
Are you trying
to "describe" me, boy?
No, no, I hastened to add.
And by the way boy
if there's any addin
to do around here
I'll do it, that's my stick
comprende?
Where's my dark ace?

Into the cord of that question
a stranger turned his brilliantined head
pulled open his fabrikoid coat
and said
            What's your business
with any dark ace!
                        The scene
became a bas-relief
as the length of the bar froze
arms and legs, belts and buckles caught
drink stilled in mid-air
Yea! You! You're a horse
aincha? I mean you!
and, "looking around," *Horseface!*
                        strum

The Stoned Horse said slowly
not looking up
from his rolling and planning
Stranger you got a pliable lip
you might get yourself described
if you keep on.
Come on!
Who's the horse, I mean who's
horse is that, we can't have
no horse! in here.
It ain't proper.
and I think I'm gonna
put a halter on you!
Uh uh, the Gunslinger breathed.
Anybody *know* the muthafucka
the Stoned Horse inquired
of the general air.
Hey, hear that the stranger gasped
that's even a *negra* horse!

Maybe so, maybe not

the Gunslinger inhaled
but stranger you got an attitude
a mile long
as his chair dropped forward
all four legs on the floor
and as the disputational 44
occurred in his hand and spun there
in that warp of relativity one sees
in the backward turning spokes
of a buckboard, then came suddenly
to rest, the barrel utterly justified
with a line pointing
to the neighborhood of infinity.
The room froze harder.
Shit,
Slinger, Lil shouted, You've pointed
your 44 straight
out of town.
I keep tellin you
not to be so goddamn fancy
now that amacher's
got the drop on you!
      Not so, Lil!
the Slinger observed.
Your vulgarity is flawless
but you are the slave
of appearances —
this Stockholder will find
that his gun cannot speak
he'll find
that he has been described

      strum

the greenhorn pulled
the trigger and his store-bought iron
coughed, and then changed

its mind, muttering
something about having
been up too late last night.
Its embarrassed handler
looked, one eye wandering,
into the barrel
and then reholstered it and
stood there.

strum

The total 44
recurred in the Slinger's hand
and spun there
then came home like a sharp knock
and the intruder was described —
a plain, unassorted white citizen.

You can go now,
the Turned On Horse said.
That investor'd make
a good janitor Lil observed,
if I was gonna keep this place
I'd hire him.
What does the foregoing mean?
I asked. Mean?
my Gunslinger laughed
Mean?
Refugee, you got some strange
obsessions, you want to know
what something *means* after you've
seen it, after you've *been* there
or were you *out* during
that time? No.
And you want some *reason.*
How fast are you
by the way? No offense

asking that is there?
No.

      I like you mi nuevo amigo
for a mortal you're exceptional
How fast are you?
Oh, average fast I suppose
or maybe a little more
than average fast I ventured.
Which means
you gotta draw.
Well, yes.
Umm, considered the Gunslinger
taking the telescope
from the Turned On Horse.
Please don't hold my shortcoming
against me oh Gunslinger
and may I inquire of you —
Inquire? he breathed
don't do *that*
Well then may I . . .
no I won't do that either
How is it then?
How can such speed be?
You make the air dark
with the beauty of your speed,
Gunslinger, the air
separates and reunites as if lightning
had cut past
leaving behind a simple experience.
How can such aching speed be.
Are you, further,
a God
or Semidiós
and therefore mortal?

      First things first
he reflected in the slit of his eyes

your attempt
is close
but let me warn you
never be close.
A mathematician from Casper Wyoming
years ago taught me that
to eliminate the draw
permits an unmatchable
speed which hangs tight
just back of the curtain
of the reality theater
down the street,
speed is not necessarily fast.
Bullets are not necessarily specific.
When the act is
so self contained
and so dazzling in itself
the target then
can disappear
in the heated tension
which is an area between here
and formerly
In some parts of the western world
men have mistakenly
called that phenomenology —
You mean, I encouraged
there is no difference
between appearance and —
"Reality?" he broke in
I never "mean", remember,
that's a *mortal* sin
and Difference I have no sense of.
That might be *your* sin
and additionally —
Don't *add,* that's my stick
the Horse said smiling.
Furthermore, the Gunslinger instructed —

More is more divine
said the Immobile Horse.
Furthermore, don't
attempt to burden me
with your encouragement
because
to go on to your second —
Don't add said the Stoned Horse —
question,
I am un semidiós.
And so you are mortal
after all said I
No mortal, you describe
yourself
I die, he said
which is not
the same as mortality,
and which is why I move
between the Sun and you
the ridge is my home
and it's why you seem
made of questions, refugee.
What's your name?
I, I answered.
That's a simple name
You're adding again said the Stoned Horse
Is it an initial?
No it is a single.

strum

       Nevertheless,
it is dangerous to be named
and makes you mortal.
If you have a name
you can be sold
you can be told

by that name leave, or come
you become, in short
a reference, or if bad luck
is large in your future
you might become an institution
which you will then mistake
for defense. I could
now place you
in a column from which
there is no escape
and down which the machine
will always recognise you.
Or a bullet might be inscribed with your name
or I could build a maze
called a social investigation
and drop you in it
your name
into it —
Please! I implored him
you terrify me.
What then, I asked
is my case? looking into
the Turned On Horse's eyes
who had his left leg resting on my shoulder.
The mortal can be described
the Gunslinger finished,
That's all mortality is
in fact.

STRUM

    Are you hungry
mortal I
the Gunslinger asked
and Yes I answered reflecting.
Well then Lil,
let's have some food

of two sorts
before we depart for Vegas.
Lil snapped
her gaudy fingers
and drink was brought
but not for the Classical Horse
who forewent drink
with a brush of his articulate hoof.

The usual he said.
Usual! There's nothin
usual about your diet Claude
Lil said, Horse chestnuts with the
spiney covering *int*act
and 38 stalks of celery
in a large bowl.
Claude I inquired —
Don't inquire boy
It can be unhealthy
pass the salt
Do you get called Claude?
Why not? Listen, I,
I'm as mortal as you
born in santa fe
of a famous dike
who spelled it
with an e too.
So your name is *not*
Heidegger after all, then
what is it? I asked.
Lévi-Strauss.
Lévi-Strauss?
Do I look like his spouse
No . . . I mean I've never
seen his wife.
You're a very observant type
Claude replied.

Well what do you do I persisted.
Don't persist.
I study the savage mind.
And what is that I asked.
That, intoned Claude leaning on my shoulder
is what you *have*
in other words, you provide
an instance
you are purely animal
sometimes purely plant
but mostly you're just a
classification, I mean it's conceivable
but so many documents
would have to be gone through
and dimensions of such *variety*
taken into account to realize what
you are, that
even if we confined ourselves
to the societies for which
the data are sufficiently full,
accurate, and comparable
among themselves
it could not be "done"
without the aid of machines.

    Got it ! the Slinger asked
Yea, I *heard* it I said
Not the same thing he said
Tell me more I said
Cool it he said. The Horse has
an interest in business,
haven't you noticed.
Noticed? I replied
Forget it he said, remember
you're just average fast.
Haven't you guessed?
The Horse is a double agent —

STRUM

Oh? But what about his name
Claude Lévi-Strauss is that —
Yes, you guessed it
a pseudonym. Don't get bugged Amigo

Strum

Here comes Lil.
OK, the Gunslinger breathed
we're ready.
Are you ready Turned On?
Hughes? I asked
Not now the Slinger said
here's Lil
Slinger! that Drifter claims
he can sing you a song.
What shimmering guesswork
my Gunslinger smiled
and beckoned to the young guitarist.

Strum

    As he travels across
the cabaret may I ask
a question? Move on he said.
Are those rounds
in the 44
of your own making?
No bullets, I rarely use
ordinary ammunition.
What then?
Straight Information.
What?
You're not ready.
Look, into each chamber

goes one bit of my repertoire
of pure information,
into each gesture, what
you call in your innocence
"the draw"
goes Some Dark Combination
and that
shocks
the eye-sockets of my enemies
registers what my enemies
can never quite recall.

        Another question.
Move.
What do you know
of Love?
Know? Nada, if
I knew it it couldn't be
Love.
Even a mortal knows that.
Then, what *is* it?
IS is not the link
it takes nine hundred years
to explain one blown
spark of Love
and you don't have
that much time Amigo.
How can you?
Leave it friend
I was with Helen,
in Egypt
witnessed messengers
turned into phantoms.

He pressed one long finger between
his eyes —
it beats me how you mortals

can think something *is*.
Hush, pues, here comes our Drifter.

STRUM

Salud, poeta
what song can you sing?
All songs but one.
A careful reply.
Then can you sing
a song of a woman
accompanied by that
your lute which this
company took to be a guitar
in their inattention.
Yes I can, but
an *Absolute* I have
here in my hand.
As yes, the Gunslinger exhaled
It's been a long time.

    The drifting singer
put one foot on a chair
and began

I shall begin he said

    the Song about a woman

    On a plane of this plain
    stood a stark colonnade
    which cast its black shadows
    in the form of a conception made
    where I first saw your love
    her elbows at angles

her elbows at black angles

her mouth
a disturbed tanager, and
in her hand an empty damajuana,
on her arm an emotion
on her ankle a band
a slender ampersand

her accent so superb
she spoke without saying
and within her eyes
were a variety
of sparkling moments
her thighs were monuments
of worked flesh
turned precisely to crush
what they will enclose
and in her manner is a hush
as if she shall enrage
with desire
with new fire
those maddened to taste
from her jewelled toes
to her swelled black mound
her startled faun
which has the earthy smell
of slightly gone
wild violets

O Fucking Infinity! O sharp organic thrust!
the Gunslinger gasped
                    and his fingers
spread across the evening air,
Let's split, *now!*
My Sun tells me we have approached
the 24th hour

Oh wake the Horse!

    Lil, will you join us
on our circuit to Vegas?
Leave this place and be done,
the stage sits at the post
its six abnormal horses driverless,
chafing their bits
their corded necks are arching
toward the journey
How far is it Claude?
                Across
two states
of mind, saith the Horse.
But from Mesilla said I
to Las Vegas — Vegas!
the Turned On Horse corrected
have you been asleep?
Must be more like
a thousand miles.
More like? he laughed
as we waited
for the Slinger
on his long knees
facing the burning hoop
as it rolled under
the swinging doors west

Mortal what do you mean
asked the Horse lounging and yawning
More Like!
how can distance
be more like.

    Thus, in the thickening vibration
our departure took shape
and Lil

the singer holding her arm
followed us out the swinging doors
and into the stage coach we got
and the Horse was leaning out
pinching the girls
distributing fake phone numbers
and baring his teeth and the singer
was whispering a lyric to Lil
who had her hand on the Slinger's knee
and he was looking at me

And the stage its taut doubletree
transfixed and luminous shot forth
and the Horse
pulling from his pocket
his dark glasses
put them on and spoke not
and by those five missionaries
Mesilla was utterly forgot.

BOOK 2

BOOK 2

This tapestry moves
as the morning lights up.
And they who are in it move
and love its moving
from sleep to Idea
born on the breathing
of a distant harmonium, To See
is their desire
as they wander estranged
through the lanes of the Tenders
of Objects
who implore this existence
for a plan and dance wideyed
provided with a schedule
of separated events
along the selvedge of time.

      Time does not consent.
This is morning
This is afternoon
This is evening
Only celebrations concur
and we concur To See
         The Universe
is One

All may wake who live
the combination is given
and Some comb the connections
in blind search
there are deaths at birth
there is death at 21
        and burial at 80
the obligation then is 101
each calculation
involves another century.

    Our company thus moves collectively
along the River Rio Grande.

    The poet starts the strings,
as sleep inhabits the stage,
along the silver of a morning raga,

        So this raga disperses
        as the shimmering of its sense
        goes out, Into the dry brilliance
        of the desert morning Along the vanes
        of the willow leaves Along the hallucination
        of the atmospheric realism Into the upper reaches
        of the Yggdrasillic yoga Over inner structure
        of the human thing like Unto the formation
        of the pinnate ash in which our treehouse sways
        and the samara goes wingéd, Oh wild Angelica!
        Oh quickbeam! oh quake and sway into waking,
        With aspergill enter Into the future

    Suddenly the doubled reflection
of a distant butte
appear in the Slingers opened eyes
He speaks the word Whitehare
and makes a wish
for the 1st day of the month and then chants

Have you noticed how everboring
the following day is,
If there be nothing new but that which is

And then he stretched
so that, sitting between the Horse
and Lil, his limbs pierced the windows
on both sides
and the stage had arms.
How like a winter hath my absence been
observed the Slinger to himself
yet unable to stifle his yawn
for his hands were with his arms
off stage.
     Aah . . . In the high west
there burns a furious Starre
It is morning

Poet, that raga is called
The Coast of the Firmament

Then you know it?

Perfectly

I dont think the Perfect
can be known.

Very good. Then you must
never consort with the Perfect,
stick to the Absolute, it's
pliable, and upon it
you seem to play any tune
you choose. Can we have
a morning song? now.
Yet first, do you sing the traditional Rock
Oh Light; The Light!

Then as the poet
fixed his 'Lute
the Slinger parted the curtains
to have a look at the stereoscopic world.
From your sweet voice
I am astoned,
before you begin, he said
as the poet began,

  Now; get this action right!
  When I say light I mean the light
  Thats the light within the light
  Thats the mornin thats the light
  Light the mornin light the light
  Thats the natchral thats all right
  Oh baby, light the mornin like the light

  Oh baby, light the morning like the night
  Put the mornin where it's tight

  Hey theres the sun hes comin in
  Theres the bird shes back again
  Make the sun hes comin up
  Make the bird shes gonna sing
  Turn your head, dig let it rang

  Oh baby douse the funky night
  Put the mornin where it's tight.

A roll of Solar Reality,
my friend, your mind
is marvelously heliocentric
your fingers have been brushed
by the fleece on Aries flank.

Thus,
I see we are yet some distance

outside Universe City, will you please
then, draw your fingers
across a variation of the line
"Cool Liquid Comes"
so that the roots of my soul
may be loosened and grow past
the hardness of the Future.

The poet turned the claws
of the Golden Griffin
of his pure lute
and absolved the strings.
I hope I can make that he breathed.

Cool Liquid Comes
he whispered
and grazed an ascension
of notes, and sang

      Cool liquid comes
      the morning . . . sensing . . .
      the morning sensing Inne
      the blend of spatial hours
      cool blending comes

      Comes blending the arc
      comes gripping urge timing
      the   blanching
                    the plain

      branding morning
      on the worlds side
      the great plaining zodiacus

      The great brand of our crossing
      the fabulous accounting
      of our coursing

the country of our consciousness

Cool comes the greatness
the scalar beauty intointoo
oh our morning bright environment
along the passage of our company
into the hoodoos
lying around the foot of our future

Cool flight along our trail
comes a rupture of feathers,
Laterally comes the desert lark
throat of memory of an extinct tree
into the light of afterdark
gone out to the dry sea in bateaux

Cool dry,
Shall come the results of inquiry
out of the larks throat
oh people of the coming stage
out of the larks throat
loom the hoodoos
beyond the canyon country

Oh temptation of survival
oh lusterless hope
of victory in opposites

Cool Liquid, cool liquid distilled
of the scalar astral spirit
morning sensing congealing
our way, hours of spatial cooling
weighing the lark appealing

Oh Narrowness of protestation!

And oh in the cool lateral morning even

in the cool wide burn of
our œnanthic unrest and willfullness
we move west and no more
Shall Dawn Bless our Altar Cloth

Aye singer. O absolutist.
You have sung a spelling account
of this Zone, yet
what a way to begin the morning !
Aye, Aye, you have lyricd
somewhat predestinarian
as all things of the imagination
must be. Thank you nomad,
for that cool rendering
of the Panorama.

　　The singer took away
the yellow rose
from his pleated blousecuff
and presented it
to the morning wind
then turned to adjust his astrolabe
and applied the oil of Atropine
to its working parts.
Andromeda turns and flashs
on the far shore, he observed.

The Slinger crossed his sheathéd legs
and pulling on his vest
fastened the mescal buttons
thereon and truly turned his eyes
into the landscape, Who
is this? he asked.

Is that an abstract question?

No. it seems material

but we'll know more
if the horses choose to stop.

What can you see then
with the sun on our left
in this vacuum of social infinity
that you blink your eyes so?
asked the poet

When most I wink then do mine eyes best see.
A man appears. He gestures
with his thumb. The six driverless horses
are inquisitive, they draw to a stop.

Wayfarer,
Have you a name
for Fate to use
when she pulls the end of your time
off the spool?

Yes. A birth Pang
from my mothers mind

A diacritical remark,
What is it?

Cool Everything.

   We Did!
several miles back
awoke and spoke the Horse
yawning thru the awning.)

Your surname I find hard
to place, its *generalness*
is overwhelming.

My fathers seed burst away
as the autumn dispersal
of a milkweed pod
conveying me into my mothers womb
via the wind.

A windy beginning!
What is the name of your throat?

Huh!?

You have introduced your thumb
yet omitted his name

Man I dont know where youre at
I'm just hitchhiking
to Universe City and beyond
Where you going?

Universe City.

Can I have a ride?

That was assumed gesturelessly
the six driverless horses
stop only to pick up.
What keeps you beside the road?

Dispersal, friend
my Head has been misplaced.

Then climb in
and get yourself together
we approach the outskirts.

     Our company moves once more
in the swift running coach

across the sparkling morning
thru the sharp rising scent
of the sage scattered river hills.

And in the Yellow Rose of Dawn
Miss Lil reads her encyclopaedia
in a slender handled mirror
held before her
in her exquisitely strung hand
and reaffirms
that ancient arrangement of amaranthine flesh
the quick aniline of flawless brow
the pure full readyness of her lips
the open public amazement of her silken cheek,
And I shall turn, into a Bluebird
she sings to the breeze and then
with some smiles she arrives at the dock
in a Masserati and boards the ship of Dawn.

Smoke? asked Everything
offering the lady his jewel studded bag.

What it is?

Tobacco.

No thank you. What's your name.

Cool Everything.

You better stay away from tobacco
or you might do just that, Pardner.

What happened to I she asked
his eyes dont seem right.

I is dead, the poet said.

That aint grammatical, Poet.

Maybe. However Certain it seems,
look, theres no reaction.

Shake him no more then!
requested the Gunslinger,
we'll keep him with us
for a past reference
Thus are his cheeks the map of days outworn,
Having plowed the ground
I has turned at the end of the row
a truly inherent *versus*
.daeha sa kcab emas eht si I ecnis

Thus, this poor individual
like all the singulars of his race
came in forward and goes out sternward
and some distant starre flashes even him
an indiscriminate salute.

That sounds deep, Slinger
But it makes me sad
to see I go, he was,
I mean *I* was so perplexed
I's obsessions were almost real
me and I had an understanding
I dont like to see I die.

I dont wish to distract you
with the metaphysics of the situation Lil
yet be assured,
I aint dead.

I *know* that, Slinger.
It's possible you missed it
the Slinger allowed,

I speak of *I*
Him? Lil pointed.
Is that not I? Stilled
inside whoever he is.
Oh. Well I'll be . . .
We never knew anything much
about him did we. I
was the name he answered to,
and that was what he had
wanderin around inside him
askin so many questions
his eyes had already answered
But wheres he at
If I aint dead?

     Life and Death
are attributes of the Soul
not of things. The Ego
is costumed as the road manager
of the soul, every time
the soul plays a date in another town
I goes ahead to set up
the bleechers, or book the hall
as they now have it,
the phenomenon is reported by the phrase
I got there ahead of myself
I got there ahead of my I
is the fact
which not a few anxious mortals
misread as intuition. The Tibetans
have a treatise on that subjection.
Yet the sad fact is I is
part of the thing
and can never leave it.
This alone constitutes
the reality of ghosts.
Therefore I is not dead.

Imagine that, Lil said
patting I's stiff knee.

We wont have to Everything offered
it's gonna be hot soon.
I only mean I never met I
but if he turns out to be put together
like most people I's gonna
come apart in the heat.
You see what I mean?

The boy has a point Slinger
it could get close fast in here.

     Yes, reflected the Poet
As the Yellow Rose of Dawn climbs
he loses the light azimuthal fragrance of his arrival
and becomes a zenith
of aparticular attention—
All Systems Go.
There will be some along our way
to claim I stinks.

The Slinger considered this
conference of voices
yet could relate very little
to the realness
of the engendering emergency.
Since I am extraTerrestrial he said
I have no practical sense of smell.

     More likely you can't keep your nose
out of those $50 bags,
observed the Horse. Anyway
we can drop it off at a bus stop
as we go thru Albuquerque
that populationll never know the difference.

I would urge you, friends.
I is a reference to the past
and cannot be so dropped
If I stinks, it is only thus
we shall not so easily forget.

Perhaps the Slinger signals a detour
past a probable and dangerous lapse
counseled the Singer. By the way
Everything, what have you
in that 5 gallon gas can?

Huh!? oh that.
well thats, uh,
Acid.

How pure is it?

Straight man.
1000 percent,
nothin but molecules.

Will you pour a little on this
and the Poet took away from his blousecuff
the Supreme Colorless Rose
of Noon
and held it under the spout.

Thank you, Cool.
The poet then presented
the Rose to his nose
and sniffed the autotheistic chemical
What subtle richness he whispered
this would turn one into an allegory
and after an inordinately long time
he observed all eyes upon him
and said I believe,

not that it matters,
this to be our solution
the perceptual index
of Everythings batch
is High, to say the least.
What then, if we make I
a receptacle of what
Everything has,
our gain will be twofold,
we will have the thing
we wish to keep
as the container of the solution
we wish to hold
a gauge in other words
in the form of man.
It is a derangement of considerable antiquity.

Instead of furmaldahyde?
Lil asked

Exactly, replied the poet.

What will that do to I
and what will it do
to my uncut batch
Everything wondered.

Only Time can reveal the immaterial
the poet said, rolling up
I's sleeve, at the same time
hanging the 5 gallon can spout down
from the ceiling of the coach
and adjusting the tubes.

I wont hold 5 gallons
Everything said as tho
he'd thot of a hitch.

I will the poet answered
we'll use his stomach too,
and elaborated,
All that I will hold
we will put into him.

That, observed the Slinger
is where your race
put its money.

Advice is common, answered the poet
the race is not over.

Well said, breathed the Slinger.

    We're inside
the outskirts, announced the Horse,
a creature of grass and only marginally
attracted to other distortions.
Here we are in the sheds
and huts of the suburbs. There are
some rigid types in here.
It's kinda poignant
but that doesnt move it any closer to the center.
Yup! empty now of all but a few
stubborn housewives
and disturbed only by the return
of several husbands known to be unable
to stay away during this celestial repast
called lunch. Thats where youre out
before you leave. Theres a man
turning on his sprinkler, it should be illegal
a small spray to maintain his grass, the Edible
variety no one doubts.
But I see none of my friends grazing there
these green plots
must be distress signals to God

that he might notice
their support of one of his minor proposals
He must be taken by these remote citizens
to be the Patron of Grass.
Holy shit, Lawn grass . . .
from that great tribe
they selected something to *Mow*

And the Horse came apart laughing
pounding his belly so that the coach swayed
and rocked from the shifting about
of his 14 hundred pounds. Hey Horse!
Cool that movement Cool demanded
youre gonna loosen all the connections!
youre gonna spill the cargo!

Dont lower the Horse,
Gunslinger admonished Everything
He has a pure Head.
It's a rare thing these days. *And*
Our mission is to encourage the Purity of the Head
pray we dont lose track of our goal.

Sorry Horse, Cool said gently
I lost my head.

Forget it Everything, youve got
a lot on your mind. Here, have a chew
off my plug.

Is that Tennessee roughcut?

No, it's Pakistani Black.

Thanks. It exudes the sweat of young boys.

I wouldnt appreciate that.

The Slingers right I guess, I am
a pure head. Here, let me help you
with those tubes.

No, No, thats ok
it's kinda delicate work.

And when, the grass comes u-up
sang the Horse

>   And when the grass goes dow-own
>   And when, the fair yong sor-rel
>   lies in the green green tow-own
>   the para-dice will floo-rish
>   And we'll be moving gra-zing
>   in the wind, oh in-to the oowind.
>   And when, the grass comes u-up
>   and *when* the wind goes dow-own
>   We'll *Flash* on our own legs then
>   and nev-er-more come dow-own

An Equestrial song Horse,
I'm moved next to your race by its beauty,
the poet related with a look of sadness,
I hope you make it.

The Gunslingers eyes were covered
with his slender fingers.
I'm al*right* Lil whispered
when the hand of Everything
touched her shoulder, I'm
just looking for my handkerchief.

Wow, this is a strange group,
Everything breathed.

There was the faintest semblance

of a smile on I's posthumous mouth.

    The Poet took away
from his embroidered lapel
the Rose of High Noon
too intense to be seen
too bright to be identified by color
and with a sigh of regret
presented it to the rising thermal dust
where it became inset
in the scrolls of the precious atmosphere.

    We're *Here!* laughed Everything

Sounds like an adverb
disguised as a place, commented the Slinger

What?

Sounds like an adventure.

Oh, yea, man I *never thot* I'd see this place.

Then you'll have the privilege of seeing it
without having thot it, prompted the Slinger.

Let's have Lunch, said Lil,
I'm starved.

Then youre beyond the hand of Lunch
diagnosed the Slinger

Scheduled food is invariably tasteless
said the Poet.

Yet in the desert
you'd be happy to eat the schedule itself

61

the Slinger finished.

    And so, they all decoached
in Old Town. And having touched
their soles to terra firma
they all stood deeply and fully struck
and their physical peripheries grew so dumb
that they appeared studiously normal
when I decoached unaided
and attended only by an attitude
of such expensive conception
he seemed the offspring of a thousand laboratories.

I has shot past mortification
whispered the Slinger

I carries the Broken Code
the key to proprioception,
is it possible he has become the pure Come
of become, asked the Poet
of the Slinger's ear.

Would you put that into my ear
another way?

Por nada.
I is now an organ Ization
a pure containment
He has become a Five, Gallon, Can
I is now a living Batch

Me heard you the First time
the Slinger nodded
thats a Very interesting tautology.

    The Tautology walked
from the stage step to the hitching post

and there stroked the manes
of the six driverless horses, latherbathed and steaming.

Thats never before been done, Slinger breathed

Whats happening to my batch, Cool enquired

Your batch is now The batch
expropriation is accomplished
we stand before an original moment
in ontological history, the self, with one grab
has acquired a capital S, mark the date
the Gunslinger instructed,
we'll send a telegram to Parmenides.

That shits not gonna help me, Cool Everything exploded
I was going to retire on that batch !

I has, the Slinger corrected,
at which Everything fell to the ground.

Our company reassembled itself
and followed I with a triple impression—
for now they sought
to keep track of what they Had,
invested in where it Was,
and carried by where it's At

We need help, the Poet reckoned.

A band of citizens had gathered.
They blocked the way. They too
were meshed with the appearance of I
Tho their interest was inessentially
soldered to the surface, and tho
they had nought invested, an old appetite
for the destruction of the Strange

governed the massed impulse of their tongues
for they could never comprehend
what the container contained.
Whats That! they shouted
Why are his eyes turned north?
Why are his pants short on one side?
Why does his hair point south?
Why do his knees laugh?
How does his hat stay on?
Wherez his ears?
The feathers around his ankle!
What does his belt buckle say,
What do his shoes say,
we cant hear them!
Why dont his socks agree!
Theres a truckpatch in his belly button
does he have a desire to grow turnips?!
He hasnt bought a license for his armpits!
Look! they shouted,
his *name* is missing
from his shirt pocket
and his managers name
is missing from his back,
He must be a Monster! Look
His pocket meters show Red
and they all laughed and screamed
This Vagrant, they shouted,
has got *nothing,* has no *cash*
and *no card,* he hasn't got a *Pot . . .*

Into the dead center of this ellipsis
the Slinger shot a complex gesture
and his mouth worked feverishly
thru the data of a forgotten alphabet
and his eye tracked smoothly toward the East
and there was produced in I's right hand
a Pot, and in his left hand *a Window*

exactly between the citizens voices
. . . to piss in or a window
like when the plug is pulled on the record player.

    Whereupon the Slinger
with a bow of *great* elaboration
and Immense profundity
turned to the half crazed crowd and said
I thank you, kind people,
for your lunchtime welcome,
you have greeted us with a kiwanis enthusiasm
we have been welcomed by Lions
as the sign outside your town predicted.

Witchcraft ! shouted a man deep inside the crowd
and was instantly conveyed to within one inch
of the Slingers nose
by an arm become a boom, its fingers
encircling the mans neck—You are correct
citizen, your identification is the *same*
as your word for fear !

Huh ? ! Put me down !

Whereupon the Slinger opened his fingers,
and the citizen dropped into the dust.

    So this is Universe City
Lil annotated.

So it is, echoed Everything.
Used to be called Truth or Consequences
they ordered the truth
and got shipped the consequences
One of their mainstreet thinkers
must have thot they could make it back
with something Large—thats howcome

it looks like a rundown movie lot
a population waiting around to become
White Extras. Wide spots in the road
have a tendency to get wider
due to the weight and speed
of the traffic going thruem.

Isnt that Interesting
Lil thot
as if she were not listening.

                    Everything tugged
at the Slingers embroidered sleeve
Hey, now that you dealt the crowd
a queer hand
why dont we have a walk around the plaza
stretch our legs, pan the scene
you know, get it Right,
we dont wanna go straight into an automatic scarf
Let's dig it, exercise—shoot some grass.

You have an impeccable sense
of everything, including
the next step, the Slinger had to say.

Yeah, well thats because
I think I saw Dick Tracy
descend in a bucket with crutches.

Is that an alarm?

No man it's a fact.
Now he's walkin toward us
trying to get on the soundtrack
of a flick titled Reality
but look! some wit stamped Crime Watcher
on his forehead when he wasnt lookin

66

Let's move!

Hang light, Cool,
the earth moves beneath your feet
like a ball bearing.

The travelers drift easily
around the plaza, I
examines the jewelery of the native women
with the rhythmic patience of Eternity.
He gradually drops behind.

The poet accompanies Lil
and guides her meanderings
over the civilian and pseudo-historic terrain
as if he had spent late hours
pouring over charts.

The Horse evangelizes
now and again
the reinchecked horses
of the plaza, bringing news
beyond the heads of most of them. Still,
One big white runs off immediately
when it is explained to her the reins
are not fixed to the ground,
and into the ear of a tall black
standing in front of the saloon
the message ran straight and clear.

This horse laughed out loud
and tore the finely tooled saddle
off his back by hooking the belly strap
on a knot in the hitching rail
whereupon he seized the pommel
with his great teeth and pitched
the whole affair thru the swinging doors

leaving one of them banging
off one hinge. A loud
vacuum of pure silence
flowed suddenly forth
from that busy place.

And in its wake,
with a punctuality almost
beyond relief, appeared the owner
of the saddle
and the horse
guns in both hands
cigar between teeth
hat on head sideways
his face a miracle of undocumented
attention, his eyes
engaged in full count down
his head is a spasm
of presyntactic metalinguistic urgency

What What What
Where Where Where
Who What Where
What Where Who

Someone conducts a search
for pure social data
a quest abstracter than Parsifals
the Slinger commented
as his group strolled past the scene.

I dont think so the stoned Horse said
This owner seeks a chimaera

What a difficult target to find
The Slinger smiled
I havent seen one since December

And thats gone north for the Winter
the Horse reckoned

     Immediately these words
out of the Horses mouth were out
the enraged Owner discharged
ten rounds with such ferocious rapidity
the bullets got stuck back to front
crowding each other out of the barrel
and fell to the boardwalk
as two segmented slugs 12345
each about $2\frac{1}{2}$ inches in length.
Plunk Plunk said Cool Everything
and picked up one of the formations
and handed it to the Slinger who spoke on it

Brilliant. I'm sure Ive never seen
the result of such ferocity, a stutter
of some deep somatic conflict, this owner
was ill-advised to use a gun at all
and least of all to let it speak for him.

You see, he continued
turning to Lil and the Poet
this can only be
materialism, the result
of merely *real* speed. All
the smoothest gunnies Ive known
were metaphysicians and of course
no jammonings of this sort were ever
associated with their efforts
and the slug was then handed to the poet.

A timejam of some crudeness
observed the poet, the bullets are dead
lead has been renderd to lead.

Yes, lead is a Heavy metal
the Slinger agreed, Whats that Crunch?
Everything asked and the group
turned in time to see
the Owners guns fall to pieces
in the same instant the Owners hulk
powdered, the ferrament altogether crushed
at the same the Owners hulk
settled into a sort of permanence
as if a ship, gone to the bottom
shifts several ways into the sand
while finding her millennial restingplace.

    It has become an Old Rugged Statue
of the good ol days, Everything gasped
a summary of accounts compiled
from frontier newspapers,
it must be worth a pile do you think
we should auction it? On the spot
answered the Horse who had a gavel
and began to pound upon a barrel
Do I hear a dollar, and he heard a dollar
and since money speaks the company left him
at the direction of a lively scene.

    Cool Everything promenaded
with the Slinger and bent his ear
toward a piece of Explanation picked up
from an hand bill he found
on the ground where the stage stopped

    This kinda flick sounds new.
It's a revolutionary medium
It's sure to turn everything around.

Sounds as tho it's meant only for you
commented the Slinger

Thats the trouble with a name like mine
What I mean is Everybody—
A tangible change, the Slinger noticed.

Everybodys *got* to see this

Is all the world a cinema then?
Name this thing.

Well, There's like a Literate Projector,
right?, which,
when a 35 mm flick is put thru it
turns it into a Script
Instantaneously!
and projects that— the finished script
onto the white virgin screen
and theyre gonna run it
in Universe City tonight

Is there no more
to this Reversal asked the Slinger.

Yea, sounds like a wild turnaround
it will Invent a whole new literachure
which was already there
a lot of big novels will get restored
in fact Everything, uh, I mean
all of it can be run the other way
some of the technikalities
havent been worked out for documentaries
but let's face it, Right?
you could rerun I mean all of it
Dig—Shoot a volcano, project it
and See the Idea behind it
sit down at the geologic conference
and hear the reasons Why
skip the rumble, move into the inference.

Eventually you could work your way back
to where it's still really dark
all the way back of the Brain?
Dig it?

Hows it powered?

2 hundred and 40 shots
into the same instant
any outlet, man.

Every outlet?

No, just any.
Theres no color of course
It's gonna be a black and white script
even when it's a color film,
you see, parrots dont show up

Hows that?

Well, I'm not sure, handbill dont say.
Colors kinda complex, probly can't
get it together intime to send it the other way
it's got something to do with reality
you dig?

Forever, inhaled the Slinger

See! theres the marquee

LITERATE PROJECTOR

We gotta make that tonight—
and get this
They can distort the Projector
so that the script Departs

from the film, in Front!
of the First Word, now man
thats complex, every day is payday
like April 1st!

There is but one Logos
tho many Images audition
the Slinger intervened.

What?!

Resume your Ontology, Everything.

Ontology? Man I'm just
telling you a story
about this projector, thats all.

My medium friend, nothing
which is demonstrative, as
this L.P. seems to be,
is ever All, for one thing
it is locked on this Side
of the Beginning, Toward what
are you pointing by so speaking
of the projector as the Sunne
and the Script as Holy Writ?

Crazy, in other images
this machine makes it possible
for people who can't make films
to produce scripts and,
as the author of the handbill
is at some pains to point out
it was designed for the stix
but works best in University towns
and other natural centers of doubletalk.
To put it in another can

the Literate Projector
enables to user to fail insignificantly
and at the same time show up
behind a vocablulary of How It is
Shake a circus up and down
put funny music next to Death
Or document something
about military committment
and let woodchucks play the parts
so say something quick about the war
in, well you know where the war is.

Like who and like who?
the Slinger tested.

Like Jonas Mekas and like Robert Krammer
Everything snapped his fingers twice
at random.
The point is it has to be read
to be seen, and like if the accent
is so incomprehensible and hysterical
it can only be coming from inside
the cinerama of the 3rd Reich
youre just not supposed to hear it.

Like as the waves make toward the Pebbled shore
Quoth the Slinger
What were you doing on December 7th?

I wasnt born then.

Nevertheless we must witness this phenomenon
We must have a *Littoral* instance.

I didnt know you had a drawl, Slinger

I dont, I slow up at noon

from the inertia of National Lunch
and from the scatteredness
of the apexed sun which attempts
at that point to enter a paradox—
namely, The West which is The East.

You say the Sun moves!?

Not exactly. Yet when I say
what I say,
The Earth Turns.

UmmUm. That's *Big,* Everything reflected

No *Local Parallels,* admitted the Slinger.
Look ye Everything,
is that a heavy-duty worker
I see at the newstand laughing
into a copy of Scientific American?

It appears so, Master Slinger.

Then we'll question him, here
he is :
            How, dreamer,
        will fate mark you
in her index when she comes dressed
as a crystalographer
to religne the tumblers
inside your genetic padlock?

How's that?

He wants to know your name.

Ah yes, how foolish of me,
Dr. Flamboyant, Dr. Jean Flamboyant

I was the flame of my Lyceum
I can fix anything

Anything? said Everything

Anything. Would you like a light
I see your roach has gone out
continued the Doctor Catching his breath

Slinger, did you dig how
the PHD caught his breath,
never saw anybody do it with their hand

Yes agreed the Slinger, Brilliantly fast
Uh thank you puffed the Slinger
youre very polite, Did,
Thanks! Did you take a degree?

May I sit down asked the doctor
fanning his neck
with the Scientific American
and motioning to a bench.

Prie Dieu! the Slinger gestured
with his long fingers, scattering
half the population of the plaza.

Thats right (tho I didn't know it was missed
I *took* a degree
which they had refused to *give* to me.

Oh?

Yes. They couldnt locate the . . .
the Object
of my dissertation :
The Tensile Strength of Last Winter's Icicles.

You must be joking.

Not at all, it was
that conjectural—
it's whats called
a post-ephemeral subject,
always a day late, their error lay of course
in looking for an object.

Ah Yes the Slinger mused
tracking with the Poet
the yellow moon's ascent
When it get *to you*
them in their case, me
in mine,
it doesnt exist
like the star whose ray
announces the disappearance
of its master by the presence of itself.

Correct! That is, within the limits of analogy.

Excellent, *Excellent*. Will you join us
Doctor, as we circle the square
of this plaza?

May I accompany you?

As you wish, flourished the Slinger
committing 3000 crows to rise
from their roosts in the cottonwoods.

And so they continued
to walk and to talk
and to discourse on
the parameters of reality.

And by this process they arrived
at the door of the printers just in time
to greet the Horse quitting
that establishment with a bundle
of parchment.

Hello Horse,
How'd the Auction
go, Cool asked

Not Bad Not Bad
the Horse laughed
There was some figurante
standin there in a bucket
with crutchs,
he was a "Lucky-Strike Green" fan
so I got the Tall Black
to start a rumor about the statue
was a Warhol disguise
and the fan jumped the bid
from 10 dollars to 20,000

Dollars? !

No. Thats the funny part.
Pounds; this fan was covered
so many ways he got confused.

Crazy. What happened then?

Well Nothin. It stayed there
Sold to the man in the bucket
with crutchs. I mean
no local was gonna raise that.
So he straps it to the bucket
and takes off.
By the way Slinger

that printers a local printer.

Makes sense, answered the Slinger.

The Horse then left the scene
and began to nail his parchments
around the plaza.

.

PROCLAMATION

RE: *the Cycle of Robart's Wallet* to
the citizens of U. C.: There is in your
city today an Illustrious Traveller whose
Earthname is Gunslinger and whose
Image you have seen an hour ago
decoach at the SouthWest corner of the
pigsty you call your Plaza. The Gun-
slinger having turned the condition of
the local citizenry around as he turned
himself around the Pigpen you call your
plaza has concluded that the prescrip-
tion for your sick heads can best be filled
by your personal attendance five minutes
hence in the Tanner's yard at the S.E.
corner of this "plaza" to see the poet
recite the above allusion. Your presence
is more than required.

Does that mean we dont have to go
asked one clever voter
of the Horse.

That's *right*, answered the Horse
studying the voter.
If youre as clever as your question indicates
you can stick a six cent stamp
on your head
and send it thru the mail—we'll process it
as soon as possible.
But if youre not, I'd advise you
to get your head over there
just like the proclamation says!